SEPT. 11, 2001

A Time for Heroes

A Tribute to American Faith, Guts, and Patriotism

Lance Wubbels

TREASURE HOUSE

P.O. Box 310
Shippensburg, PA 17257-0310
www.destinyimage.com

Treasure House

An Imprint of
Destiny Image® Publishers, Inc.
P.O. Box 310
Shippensburg, PA 17257-0310

"For where your treasure is, there will your heart be also."
MATTHEW 6:21

ISBN 0-7684-3046-1
For Worldwide Distribution
Printed in the U.S.A.

This book and all other Destiny Image, Revival Press, MercyPlace,
Fresh Bread, Destiny Image Fiction, and Treasure House books are available
to Christian bookstores and distributors worldwide.

For the U.S. bookstore nearest you, call **1-800-722-6774**.
For more information on foreign distributors, call **717-532-3040**.
Or reach us on the Internet at **www.destinyimage.com**

To Our Heroes

The Brave and Courageous

Who Walk Through Fear

No Matter the Price

LANCE WUBBELS is presently the Vice President of Literary Development at Koechel Peterson & Associates. For the previous eighteen years, he worked as the Managing Editor of Bethany House Publishers as well as a teacher at Bethany College of Missions.

A naturally gifted storyteller, Wubbels is the author of seven fiction books with Bethany House Publishers. He won the Angel Award for *One Small Miracle*, the heartwarming novel about the profound impact of a teacher's gift of love on the life of one of her struggling students. He has also compiled and edited twenty-five Christian Living Classic books published by Emerald Books. His daily devotional, *In His Presence*, won the 1999 Gold Medallion Award from the Evangelical Christian Publishers Association.

He and his family make their home in Bloomington, Minnesota.

CONTENTS

*Greater love
has no one than this,
that he lay down his life
for his friends.*

JESUS CHRIST

JOHN 15:13

A TIME FOR COURAGE

*These acts of mass murder
were intended to frighten
our nation into chaos and retreat,
but they have failed.*

Our country is strong.

*Terrorist acts can shake
the foundation of our biggest buildings,
but they cannot touch
the foundation of America.*

PRESIDENT GEORGE W. BUSH

SEPTEMBER 11, 2001

A TIME TO WEEP

My country, 'tis of thee,
Sweet land of liberty,
Of thee I sing:
Land where my fathers died,
Land of the pilgrims' pride,
From every mountainside
Let freedom ring.

SAMUEL FRANCIS SMITH

"AMERICA," 1831

September 11, 2001

8:40 A.M. (EST)

I am driving on the freeway to work, listening to some meaningless banter about Senator Gary Condit on talk radio.

8:45 A.M.

One of the talk radio personalities suddenly breaks their conversation with a report he's watching on *CNN*. A plane, he says, has apparently crashed into one of the World Trade Center towers in New York City. My first thought was disbelief, figuring that a small commuter plane must have veered off course somehow. But how does a pilot not see a building that huge on a clear day? It turns out it was American Airlines Flight 11, a Boeing 767 that left Boston for Los Angeles with eighty-one passengers and eleven crew members, that struck the Center's north tower.

8:59 A.M.

The radio station has broken away to national news coverage, and the report is that it was a commercial jet that hit the tower. "Oh, God, no," I whisper to myself, thinking of the people in the plane and in the offices, still certain it must be a small commercial jet. I call my wife at her office and tell her to turn on her radio or try to find a television to see what's going on.

9:06 A.M.

The report is that a second commercial jet has barreled into the south tower of the World Trade Center. I gasp and feel numb, immediately aware that this is no accident, but it's beyond belief, too preposterous to imagine. This was United Airlines Flight 175, a

Boeing 767 that left Boston for Los Angeles with fifty-six passengers and nine crew members.

9:12 A.M.

My wife calls me as I pull into the parking lot at work. She is in utter shock. I grab my stuff, run into the office, and join some of my co-workers around a television in one of the offices. One of them is visibly frightened. The sight of the two magnificent glass towers with their upper floors ablaze, smoke billowing out the shattered sides, is a nightmare. My breath is short and my heart is racing.

9:31 A.M.

President Bush makes a brief statement, promising that the United States will hunt down the terrorists. No one is talking in our office, except for short exclamations. I am pacing the hardwood floor.

9:40 A.M.

A third reported crash. This one at the Pentagon. A first report indicated it might be a military helicopter that was seen over the air space shortly before the crash. But a second report is that it was another commercial jet. We now know it was a Boeing 757, American Flight 77, which took off from Dulles Airport near Washington and was bound for Los Angeles.

9:48 A.M.

The West Wing of the White House is evacuated, and eventually State and Justice offices as well as all federal office buildings. Reports of other planes are being sounded, and Secret Service officers patrol Lafayette Park, across from the White House, with automatic weapons. Vice President Cheney, his wife, and Laura Bush are hurried away to a bunker on the White House grounds.

More co-workers are streaming into our office to watch. One of them is crying softly; all are agitated. Everyone is wondering what target might be next.

9:49 A.M.

For the first time in our country's history, the Federal Aviation Administration bans all aircraft takeoffs across the country.

10:00 A.M.

In what is easily the most horrible sight I have ever witnessed, the south tower of the World Trade Center suddenly shudders, as though it's been skillfully imploded, and collapses . . . seems to just disintegrate from view . . . in a volcanic-like plume of smoke and dust. The terrorists who tried to bring it down in 1993 and said the day would come when they would get it have fulfilled their word.

I am so aghast I can't breathe, and I feel the blood draining from my head. I want to look away from the television screen, but I can't. Irrationally, I hope that when the dust clears, the tower will still be there. It just has to be there. But I know it's gone, and I know that there had to be thousands of people inside. All I can do is pray. Tears begin to streak down my face, and I pace again.

I call home to see if my nineteen-year-old son is watching the news. He is, but we do not talk. I'm too upset, and I want to hear the news reports.

10:10 A.M.

There's an unconfirmed report that a fourth commercial jet has crashed in a field in Pennsylvania. I hope it's not true, but given what's happened, I'm sure it is true. United Flight 93, a Boeing 757 that was bound for San Francisco from Newark, New Jersey, with thirty-seven passengers and seven crew members, has crashed about eighty miles southeast of Pittsburgh.

I feel overwhelmed with apprehension that these scenes are going to continue all over the country. In my mind I see wave after wave of kamikaze jetliners and flaming buildings and people leaping to their deaths. I step out of the office to look out another office window to make sure that the IDS Center tower in downtown Minneapolis is still standing.

10:29 A.M.

Ever since the south tower went down, I've held my breath, hoping the other one will stand. Then as though we're seeing a replay of what had already happened, the north tower of the World Trade Center collapses. My hand is over my mouth, and my mind reels against the unfathomable. "Bombs!" I gasp out loud. "They had the building set with bombs." It looked that way. It looked as though it was a combination of the crash, the fires, and strategically placed bombs. We learned later that it was the phenomenal heat of the jet fuel fire that took the buildings down.

11 A.M.

New York Mayor Rudy Giuliani calls for the evacuation of lower Manhattan. "On any given day," a television news anchor tells us, "some 200,000 people work in or visit the World Trade Center complex." We hear reports that 50,000 people might have been in the Twin Towers. How many were there today? How many got out?

I feel utterly helpless and sullen as I watch, as though I'm in a steel cage with my arms tied behind my back and I can do nothing to stop the mass murder.

11:05 A.M.

I think of my son at home and decide to pack up some office work and head home. He's leaving on the following Monday for Marine boot camp in San Diego, and I want to be with him today. Two years before he'd told me that terrorism was going to be the new world war, and that Islamic radicals would bring it to our soil. A year previously, he had signed up for the Marines with a year's college deferment, saying, "Someone will have to defend our liberty. If I'm not willing to do it, who will?" Now this. Why now?

11:45 A.M.

I arrive home and find my son watching the news with my daughter's boyfriend, who's visiting us from Ireland and is all too familiar with terrorism. President Bush has delayed his return to Washington, stopping in Louisiana. My son is calm, measured, and stoic. I am angry. My stomach is in knots.

12:15 P.M.

My twenty-two-year-old daughter arrives home from the University of Minnesota. All classes were canceled for the day. My son goes to the basement to work out, as he has the entire summer, getting himself physically ready for the Marines.

12:36 P.M.

President Bush makes his second round of remarks from a conference room at Barksdale Air Force Base, outside of Shreveport, Louisiana. "Freedom itself was attacked this morning by a faceless coward," he said. Later he was flown with fighter jets hovering beside each wing of Air Force One to the U.S. Strategic Air Command in Nebraska.

2:51 P.M.

In what I would have never dreamed possible in my lifetime, we're told that the Navy is deploying missile destroyers and other equipment to New York and Washington. The aircraft carrier U.S.S. *John F. Kennedy* and U.S.S. *George Washington* are taking up positions off the East Coast. Fighter jets are streaking down the Hudson River. Has the world really come to this? Can it get any worse?

4:00 P.M.

I haven't moved from my chair at home. I can't pull myself away from the news coverage for fear that I might miss something. The day seems to have stood still.

5:25 P.M.

After warnings that it might happen, a third building in the World Trade Center complex collapses.

7 P.M.

President Bush arrives in Washington. I hope he is safe. On a day ripe with horror, to lose our nation's leader would be too much.

8:30 P.M.

The President addresses the nation, and I feel a sense of reassurance that we will overcome this unseen enemy. I hug my son, my daughter, and my wife. And I wish I were twenty years old again. If I were, my son would not be leaving for San Diego alone.

While all of this day was unfolding, far away in a remote valley near the border of Pakistan and Afghanistan, a close friend of mine was on a personal mission. He had gone there to try to obtain permission to enter Afghanistan and assist eight foreign missionaries who were imprisoned in Kabul by the Taliban, held on charges of proselytizing. He initially heard the news of the terrorist attacks on a small shortwave radio that crackled with static.

"My first thought was of Orson Welles' *War of the Worlds*," he said. "It was beyond belief. It wasn't until later, when I got to a television, that I realized it was devastatingly true."

Having watched the events as they happened on September 11, his description of the "War of the Worlds" seems as apt as any I have heard. Something this appalling could not have been done by human beings to other defenseless human beings.

I know this now.

Every man gives his life
for what he believes.
Every woman gives her life
for what she believes.

Sometimes people believe
in little or nothing,
and yet they give their lives
to that little or nothing.

One life is all we have,
and we live it
as we believe in living it,
and then it's gone.

But to surrender to what you are
and to live without belief
is more terrible than dying—
even more terrible than dying young.

JOAN of ARC

A TIME TO SAVE

*The political leaders
with whom we are familiar
generally aspire to be superstars
rather than heroes.*

The distinction is crucial.

*Superstars strive for approbation;
heroes walk alone.*

*Superstars crave consensus;
heroes define themselves
by the judgment of a future
they see it as their task to bring about.*

*Superstars seek success in a technique
for eliciting support; heroes pursue success
as the outgrowth of inner values.*[1]

HENRY KISSINGER

A TIME TO HONOR

"Today, Our Nation Saw Evil"

PRESIDENT GEORGE W. BUSH

This day that changed our world forever began like any other. As the last of summer's pale stars sank into an ocean of blue, the crisp, sun-sweet air of another September morning greeted early risers in New York City, Boston, and Washington, D.C. Parents rushed to get their children off to school. Busy travelers rose to catch the first flights of the day, and rush-hour traffic snarled and caused its usual delays.

There was no hint of the stormy chieftain who had dispatched his airy messengers on errands of unspeakable, unthinkable suicidal horror. No warning of a battle front that would soon rise above America's eastern seaboard to unleash its deafening roar and shake the solid earth with its shock. No whisper of sinister plots or cowardly terrorists or hate beyond measure that flew on demon wings to usher in what some said looked like the end of the world.

Who could have foreseen the unfathomable images of jets slashing through tranquil blue skies and into tall towers that seemed to swallow them whole? Or of wartime streets filled with men and women fleeing for their lives in scenes reminiscent of the bombing of Dresden? Or of majestic symbols of peace and prosperity burning like candles, then suddenly buckling, one floor pancaking the one below, and disappearing . . . taking with them thousands of people in a single moment? Or of a once proud city that looked like an ash-covered cemetery encased in an eerie smoldering forest of tall steel trees?

The haunting images replay again and again in our minds, searing away at our sensibilities.

In particular, on September 11 there was no hint of impending destruction to the innocent civilians who boarded United Airlines Flight 93 in Newark, New Jersey, bound for San Francisco, California, at 8:01 A.M. in the east.

Yet out of the dark shadows of certain tragedy, staring directly into the grim face of death, emerged American heroes who rose up against their militant extremist hijackers. In the blue skies over Ohio and Pennsylvania, they willed themselves to break through the wall of their own overwhelming fear and to rush those who had taken over the plane.

But the heroes from Flight 93 were not alone on this horrendous day. In fact, they were but the first squad of what became an army of firefighters, police, paramedics, rescue workers, and ordinary citizens who voluntarily descended into hell to attempt the rescue of their fellow Americans. Young and old, all races, all religions, many of them risking their own lives, demonstrated an indomitable spirit that sent a clear message to defy the murderous enemy: *We cannot and will not give in—never!*

This book is but a small tribute to their remarkable stories and a reminder of what true heroism is. We begin with United Airlines Flight 93, where the standard for heroism was defined. Part of what happened on that flight is forever unknowable, for every eyewitness perished. Fortunately, for our sake, a handful of voices made their way to the outside world first.

The hero in history
is the individual to whom
we can justifiably attribute
preponderant influence
in determining
an issue or event
whose consequences
would have been profoundly different
if he had not acted as he did.[2]

SIDNEY HOOK

A TIME TO STAND TOGETHER

I regret that I have but one life to lose for my country.[3]

NATHAN HALE

United Airlines Flight 93

United Airlines Flight 93 in Newark, New Jersey, bound for San Francisco, California, was scheduled to depart at 8:01 A.M. (EST). Radar logs show that there was a forty-minute delay, apparently waiting for runway traffic to clear, and that the 757-200 did not take off until 8:44 A.M.

Fortunately, the flight was less than one-quarter full with its thirty-seven passengers and seven crewmembers as it flew west and climbed to 35,000 feet. Among the passengers were four young American businessmen who had never met one another, but whom many now feel were providentially brought together for this moment. Perhaps it is not coincidental that Jeremy Glick, Mark Bingham, Tom Burnett, and Todd Beamer were all in their thirties, successful, athletic, and take-charge guys.

Four other men had also boarded who were no strangers to one another. Saeed Alghamdi, Ahmed Al Haznawi, Ahmed Alnami, and Ziad Jarrah had spent a great deal of time training for this flight as a holy mission. Their sole intent was to hijack the United plane and turn it into a new form of guided missile targeted on a national landmark. Investigators believe the hijackers on all four doomed jets on September 11 had enough training, some of it acquired at flight schools in the USA, to switch the planes' courses and take aim on their targets.

The morning's flight was apparently routine, following its designated path for just over an hour west across Pennsylvania and into Ohio. Then at 9:15 A.M., according to transcripts of cockpit radio transmissions, Pilot Jason Dahl was heard screaming: "Get out of here! Get out of here!" as the terrorists overpowered him.

Some moments later, an announcement was made over the

plane's intercom in broken English with a thick Middle Eastern accent: "There is a bomb on board. This is the captain speaking. Remain in your seat. There is a bomb on board. Stay quiet. We are meeting with their demands. We are returning to the airport."[4]

Someone in the cockpit radioed the FAA and asked for a new flight plan with a final destination of Washington, D.C. Then the jet suddenly started doubling back south and east as it reached Cleveland, taking a series of sharp turns.

Cell phone conversations from Flight 93 passengers reported that three men speaking a foreign language were in the aisle with knives and box cutters. One carried a red box he claimed was a bomb. At least one person had been stabbed and perhaps killed.

Todd Beamer, one of the businessmen believed to have led a counterattack, picked up a seat-back phone, operated by GTE, and reached Lisa Jefferson, a GTE supervisor. His call was patched through to the FBI. He told her that the hijackers had moved twenty-six passengers into first class. Beamer, nine other passengers, and the five flight attendants had been ordered to sit in the back of the plane. This group probably included the four businessmen. He said that two hijackers had locked themselves into the cockpit.

Mark Bingham, thirty-one, who had his own public relations

firm in San Francisco, had raced to get on this flight so he could be back in his office for a morning conference call. He called his mother and told her about the hijacking. "I love you," he said. Mark, at six feet five, had played rugby at the University of California, Berkeley, and still played for an amateur team. He was fearless enough to run with the bulls in Pamplona, Spain, just this summer, and had once wrestled a gun away from a mugger.

Bingham is believed to have been among the passengers who tried to take Flight 93 back from the hijackers. His mother, Alice Hoglan of Saratoga, California, is certain her son was involved. "He doesn't seek out trouble," she said, "but he won't run away from it either. If he sees something wrong, he sets it right."

During the next few minutes, Thomas Burnett Jr., thirty-eight, made four calls to his wife, Deena. An executive with a medical research company and history buff who admired Teddy Roosevelt and Abraham Lincoln, Burnett had been booked on a later flight, but he rushed to get on United 93 because he missed his wife and three daughters, who were all under the age of six.

It was 9:44 A.M. Deena Burnett was serving the girls breakfast when the first call came. Her husband said one passenger had already been killed. His calls were brief, fact-gathering conversations.

Jeremy Glick called his wife, Lyzbeth, who was at her parents' house with their two-month-old daughter. Using the phone built into the seat in front of him, he held it open as Lyzbeth patched the call through to a 911 dispatcher in Poughkeepsie, New York.

The dispatcher, Lyzbeth, and her parents listened for twenty minutes as the thirty-one-year-old Glick described the hijackers. Jeremy wanted confirmation that other planes had indeed hit the Twin Towers of the World Trade Center. He was trying to piece together whether the hijackers were going to blow the plane up with their bomb or crash it into another building. Glick, a six-feet-four, 220-pound collegiate judo champion and high school wrestler, said he and others were working on a plan, whether to rush the hijackers or not. He asked Lyzbeth what he should do. Having seen the news report that a third commercial jet had crashed into the Pentagon, she finally decided, "Honey, you need to go for it."

During her fourth and final conversation with her husband, Tom, Deena Burnett begged, "Please sit down and don't draw attention to yourself."

"No," Tom replied, fully aware of the fact that hijackers had already crashed their planes into the World Trade Center. "If they're going to drive this plane into the ground, we've got to do something."

"He didn't review his life story or say good-bye or tell me wonderful things," Deena recalled later of the six-feet-two former high school quarterback. "He was taking down information, planning what they were going to do. He was problem solving, and he was going to take care of it and come on home."

Toward the end of his conversation with GTE supervisor Lisa Jefferson, Todd Beamer told her that he and others were going to "jump on" the hijacker with the bomb, who was guarding the passengers in the rear. A high school basketball and baseball star, Beamer mentioned Jeremy Glick by name. Jefferson heard shouts and commotion on the plane, and then Beamer asked her to pray the Lord's Prayer with him. He also made her promise to call his wife, Lisa, and tell her that he loved her and the children. Then he dropped the phone.

"Let's roll" were the last words he spoke. Silence followed.

At 9:58 A.M., a male passenger reached an emergency dispatcher in Pennsylvania. "We are being hijacked," he said, hiding in a bathroom. He told the dispatcher that he heard an explosion. "The plane is going down," he said.

At 10:10 A.M., United Flight 93 crashed into a defunct coal strip mine that was now a large field of dry golden grass surrounded by woods in Somerset County near Shanksville, Pennsylvania—eighty miles southeast of Pittsburgh and eighty-five miles northwest of Camp David, the presidential retreat in Maryland.

A charred hole in the ground is all that we were given on September 11 as a monument to such heroism. A few scattered fires were all that firemen found upon arrival. There was some debris hanging from trees. Small chunks of yellow honeycomb insulation. No pieces of fuselage. No bodies. Over in the woods, fifty yards away, some shirts, pants, and loose papers.

Brave American civilians, complete strangers, rose against impossible odds and tried to save the 757-200 or make certain it never reached its intended goal. In doing so, they made the ultimate sacrifice. Of the four hijacked planes, United 93 was the only one that failed to hit a targeted site.

Pennsylvania Governor Tom Ridge gave these words to the families of the victims: "They undoubtedly saved hundreds, if not thousands, of lives." And they saved America from even a darker day to add to what New York City Mayor Rudy Giuliani called "one of the most heinous acts in world history."

True heroism is remarkably sober,
very undramatic.

*True heroism is remarkably sober,
very undramatic.*

*It is not the urge to surpass all others
at whatever cost,
but the urge to serve others
at whatever cost.*[5]

ARTHUR ASHE

A TIME TO PRAY

True heroism
consists in
rising superior
to misfortune.

NAPOLEAN

The Man Who Vowed "to Do Something"

It was an unusual sight for a Tuesday evening, September 18, in Bloomington, Minnesota. It took place just a couple of miles from my home. Rows of candles and American flags lined the entrance to St. Edward's Catholic Church. As the mourners arrived, over forty people had gathered across the street to wave flags in solemn tribute.

They came by the hundreds to honor the man they called a hero. Thomas Burnett Jr., the thirty-eight-year-old man who is believed to have helped thwart the hijackers of United Flight 93, was a Minnesota native, who lived in San Ramon, California, with his wife and three daughters. He went to the same high school that my children attended some years later. Over 1,200 friends, neighbors, family members, and even strangers filled the church.

Entering the church, one got an immediate sense of the man, Tom Burnett. There was the photo of him in his Jefferson High School football jersey from 1980 when he led the team to the state finals as their quarterback. Pictures of him as a boy blowing out birthday candles and proudly holding fish he caught on summer vacations. And there were the photos of him dancing with his wife, Deena, on their wedding day and holding twin baby daughters in his arms.

To watch the family enter the sanctuary was gut-wrenching. Three young daughters, five-year-old twins and a three-year-old, ribbons in their hair, matching blue dresses and shiny black shoes. When told that their father had died and was in heaven, the youngest asked, "Why does he want to be with Jesus instead of us?"[6] One of the twins asked if she could call him on his cell phone. The other twin asked whether the postman might take a letter to him.

And there was Tom's loving wife, Deena, who held on to the

telephone for three hours after Tom's final call, hoping for his familiar voice one more time. A father who had been Tom's best man at his wedding. A grieving mother whom Tom loved to swim with as a boy. The younger sister whom he had taught how to throw a football. An older sister who in her eulogy said, "In the course of this week, someone who to me has been very life-sized has become larger than life."[7]

Burnett was the senior vice president and chief operating office of Thoratec Corporation, a medical device company. Keith Grossman, a close friend and Tom's boss, said Tom was a man capable of taking matters into his own hands. "He is absolutely the kind of person you not only would think might be involved but you would expect to be involved. And be shocked if he wasn't." Grossman called him "exceptional. He was on his way to a truly brilliant career. I can't imagine what he would have accomplished had he had more time."[8]

But he didn't have more time. Only enough time to be the hero he already had been to his wife and daughters, family, and friends.

"Heroes," Ronald Steel said, "come along when you need them."[9] And United Airlines Flight 93 . . . and America . . . found a hero in Tom Burnett at an extraordinarily desperate moment.

Terrorists, you see, have no power over heroes.

*[The hero] finds a fork
in the historical road,
but he also helps,
so to speak,
to create it.*

*He increases the odds of success
for the alternative he chooses
by virtue of the extraordinary qualities
he brings to bear to realize on it.*[10]

SIDNEY HOOK

A TIME TO OVERCOME

Breathes there the man,
with soul so dead,
Who never to himself hath said,
This is my own,
my native land.

SIR WALTER SCOTT
The Lay of the Last Minstrel

The Man They Call a Patriot

They had been high school sweethearts, Lyzbeth and Jeremy Glick. He was the 1988 prom king and she the queen. For five years they'd been married and were the parents of a twelve-week-old daughter, Emmy. At thirty-one years of age, he was a fantastic husband and father.

To Joan and Lloyd Glick of Hewitt, New Jersey, Jeremy was a son. To Jennifer, Joanna, Jared, and Jonah he was a brother. Joanna called him a "teddy bear—just fall into his arms." And to many, many more, he was counted on as a friend.

His mother Joan said that when Jeremy was little, he was so obsessed with superheroes that he would call her "Wonder Woman." She recalls Jeremy as a boy running around the house with a bath towel tied around his neck as a cape, pretending he could fly. He picked up the nickname "Green Lantern," for the superhero who battles bad guys and fights for justice. As he grew to be six feet four, he became a high school wrestler and a national collegiate judo champion.

Three-month-old Emmy will never get the chance to know him as her father, but she will grow up with the knowledge that he was a true hero.

Jeremy had been scheduled to fly out of Newark on Monday the 10th, but he delayed it a day. Three days before the flight, he wanted to cancel the trip completely, hating to be away from home. But Lyzbeth told him that he couldn't say no to Vividence, the San Francisco Internet company where he was an executive, so he boarded United Flight 93 anyway. In an interview with Jane Pauley of NBC's *Dateline*, Lyzbeth said, "I think with all the badness going on that God or some higher power knew Jeremy had the strength to somehow stop some of the bad. I believe that. I believe that

Jeremy was meant for a higher purpose."

On that fateful Tuesday morning, Jeremy called at 7:30 A.M. to tell Lyzbeth that he was boarding the plane for the five-hour flight to San Francisco. His father-in-law, Richard Makely, answered the phone at his home in New York's Catskill Mountains, where his daughter and granddaughter Emmy were visiting. Lyzbeth was sleeping, having been up with the baby most of the night, so Richard took the message and wished Jeremy a good trip.

At approximately 9:45 A.M., Jeremy called again, and his first words were: "It's bad news. Let me talk with Lyzbeth." What followed was a twenty-minute call as the plane streaked across western Pennsylvania. It was their last conversation.

It was clear from Jeremy that three hijackers who had a bomb and knives had taken over control of the plane. The men looked to be Middle Eastern and were wearing red headbands. Jeremy believed the bomb was real, and he could tell by the plane's motion that they were circling back and were no longer bound for California.

Lyzbeth was surprised by how calm it sounded on the flight. She heard no screaming, no noises of commotion. It seemed impossible to believe that something so terrible could be happening on her husband's flight.

While they talked, Lyzbeth's mother called 911 from another phone line. Authorities from the state police patched into the call and listened to Jeremy's comments. Jeremy wanted to know what had happened at the World Trade Center, having heard about it from another passenger, probably Tom Burnett. When Lyzbeth told him it was true, he said he didn't know the hijackers' intent.

"He knew something very bad was going to happen," said Lyzbeth. "What he needed to know was what was going to happen. Were they going to blow up the plane, or was it going to crash into something else, because that made all the difference."

As they talked, Jeremy began to realize that United Flight 93 had become a guided missile for an unknown target. "My God, we're next," he said.

"We said I love you a thousand times over and over again, and it just brought so much peace to us," says Lyzbeth. "I felt the feeling from it. He told me, 'I love Emmy,' and to take care of her. Then he said, 'Whatever decisions you make in your life, I need you to be happy, and I will respect any decisions that you make.' He sounded strong. He didn't sound panicked, but very clear-headed. I told him to put a picture of me and Emmy in his head to be strong. I focused on making him know that I was OK."

The sight of the crash into the Pentagon only intensified the Glick's conversation. Jeremy and two other men were devising a plan in the back of the 757-200, which was now just a little over a half hour from the nation's capitol. Thomas Burnett had told his wife they were talking about rushing the hijackers.

Jeremy told Lyzbeth they were going to take a vote. He asked her for advice on what to do. Should they attack the terrorists? Desperately not wanting to say something wrong and have something terrible happen, she asked him if they were armed. He replied they had knives but apparently no guns. Finally, the decision came clear.

Trusting Jeremy's instincts, feeling he could do it, Lyzbeth said, "Honey, you need to do it."

Hearing her response, Jeremy joked, "OK. I have my butter knife from breakfast." And then he said, "You know, I'm going to leave the phone here. Stay on the line. I'll be back."

At that point Lyzbeth gave the phone to her father because she didn't want to hear what happened. All she could do was pray.

And so Richard Makely listened. He heard no noise for several minutes, and then there were screams in the background.

"Well, they're doing it," Richard said.

Another minute went by, which seemed like an eternity, perhaps a minute and a half, and then came another set of
screams. The noise he could hear was muffled. Then there
was nothing.

About Jeremy's actions, his mother Joan said, "I think it shows
that one person can make a difference, that one person in this
country has the opportunity to change this world and make
a difference."

"He knew that stopping them was going to end all of their
lives," said Jeremy's brother-in-law Douglas Hurwitt. "But
that was my brother-in-law. He was a take-charge guy."

Richard says, "Jeremy was a patriot."

The hero is known for achievements;
the celebrity for well-knownness.

The hero reveals the possibilities
of human nature.
The celebrity reveals the possibilities
of the press and media.

Celebrities are people who make news,
but heroes are people who make history.

Time makes heroes
but dissolves celebrities.[11]

DANIEL J. BOORSTEN

Heroism is endurance for one moment more.[12]

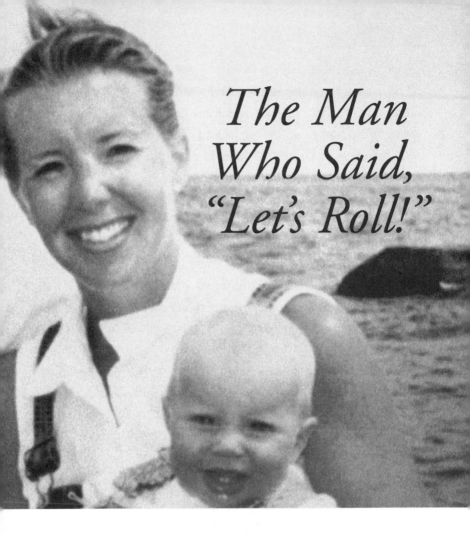

The Man Who Said, "Let's Roll!"

"Are you guys ready? Let's roll!" was an expression that Todd Beamer used all the time with his two young sons in their home in Hightstown, New Jersey.

Those were the unforgettable last words the thirty-two-year-old Sunday school teacher and account manager for the software firm Oracle said before he and others apparently rushed the hijackers of United Airlines Flight 93.

And what type of a man was he? His wife, Lisa, said that he was "the best father in the world" to their sons, David and Andrew, ages one and three. When he came home from work and she said, "Daddy's home!" the entire house would light up. "He was gentle by nature. He was also very competitive, and he wouldn't stand for anyone being hurt. He was a man of faith and action."

Todd placed a call on one of the Boeing 757-200's on-board telephones and spoke for thirteen minutes with GTE Airfone supervisor Lisa Jefferson. She patched his call through to the FBI. He was very calm and soft spoken as he provided detailed information about the hijacking. One of the hijackers appeared to have a bomb tied to his chest with a belt. He said two people were lying on the floor, whom he thought to be the pilot and copilot.

At one point, he said, "We're going down. We're going down. No, we're coming up. I don't know what way we're going. O Jesus, please help me."

Toward the end of his conversation, Todd Beamer told Robinson that he and others were going to "jump on" the hijacker with the bomb, who was guarding the passengers in the rear. "I know I'm not going to make it out of here. We're going to do something." He mentioned Jeremy Glick by name.

Before the call ended yelling and commotion were heard in the background. Beamer asked Robinson to pray the Lord's Prayer with him. Together, they recited these words: "Our Father in heaven, hallowed be your name, your kingdom come, your will be done on earth as it is in heaven. Give us today our daily bread. Forgive us our debts, as we also have forgiven our debtors. And lead us not into temptation, but deliver us from the evil one." Then he asked her to promise to call his wife of seven years, who was expecting a third child, and their two sons. "Tell her I love her and the boys."

Dropping the phone after talking with Robinson, Beamer left the line open. It was then that she heard him say, "God help me. Jesus help me. Are you guys ready? Okay, let's roll."

There were screams, then silence.

Shortly afterward, the plane crashed, killing all forty-four aboard.

"They realized they were going to die," said Lisa Beamer. "I think he thought, 'OK, I've done what I need to do, and now it's time to act.' Knowing that he helped save lives by bringing that plane down . . . it brings joy to a situation where there isn't much to be found."

*In the grossly distorted
individualism of today,
we are incapable of imagining
the selflessly disinterested hero.*

*This may not matter;
we may think we can do without him.*

*But what it also means is
that we are incapable of imagining
the selflessly disinterested hero
in ourselves who would give
himself to a cause.*[13]

HENRY FAIRLY

A TIME TO SEARCH

*A hero is someone
we can admire
without apology.*[14]

KITTY KELLEY

Who Are Our Heroes?

Many years ago, John F. Kennedy was asked how it was that he became a war hero. He responded by saying, "It was involuntary. They sank my boat."[15]

9-11-01 was a day similar to that—a day for heroes. Heroes were everywhere you looked. We saw giants rise out of relative obscurity to cast long shadows across our land. Ordinary American citizens, total strangers from all walks of life, suddenly caught in the crossfire of terrorism, put their lives on the line to preserve the lives of others.

They emerged as the truly mighty and valiant ones of Flight 93. Among the smoldering wreckage of the Pentagon, the symbol of the world's mightiest military power, they stood with undimmed spirits as firefighters unfurled a gigantic flag from the roof of the burned-out structure. And at Ground Zero, hundreds and thousands of people on dozens of fronts searched the mountain of unstable rubble in an epic battle to win back as many lives as could possibly be rescued.

Most of them remain nameless to us, but their undaunted faces are engraved forever upon our hearts. They are the firefighters, the tireless firefighters, who were forever captured by the photo of the three ashen-caked firemen raising the American flag on a pole that stuck up out of the debris of the World Trade Center. Framed against the monstrous heap of steel and concrete in the background, it was an easy reminder of the heroic Marines who raised the flag on Iwo Jima during another of this nation's great conflicts.

They are the police, paramedics, rescue workers, doctors, nurses, National Guard, Red Cross workers, and others we have so often taken for granted. And they are the janitors and security guards and office managers and the co-workers who said no to death and helped thousands escape who might have easily perished.

In that sudden moment of time, the real heroes of our world stood out as brilliant luminaries cast against the darkest night.

In a world where rock superstars, athletes, and celebrities have been elevated to hero status, we were given a lesson on true heroism. Such acts of selfless devotion are nearly beyond our imaginations. They awoke a vision of altruism we hope we are all capable of attaining.

Heroes inspire others with their bravery, their compassion, their strength, their character, and their sacrifice. Unheralded and largely unnoticed, they go about their lives of serving and protecting with responsibility and patient endurance and a sense of honor. You and I count on them being there every day no matter what. They light the way for the rest of us to follow when times are dark.

It is little wonder that the world seems so empty when they are gone.

Superman was nowhere to be found at Ground Zero on September 11. Hercules did not step in to move the mountain of destruction or untwist the snarl of steel. But hundreds of heroes stepped up to the task and quietly did the incredibly tough rescue work one piece at a time. They made the impossible begin to look possible. They helped us believe that we could go on and face whatever tomorrow might bring.

Here's to the true heroes and heroines among us. Let's not forget the mothers, fathers, grandparents, friends, teachers, coaches, pastors, and countless others who strive to make our world a better place. Who give their best that we might be the best. Who never give up when they have every reason in the world to throw in the towel.

Heroes such as we've seen and read about make us proud to be Americans. Until these recent events happened, I wouldn't have guessed that listening to "God Bless America" could make me cry. I wonder if I'll ever see the Statue of Liberty in the same light. And I hope my heart never grows dull to its patriotic meaning again.

Let us never take our heroes for granted again, and may we pray to live up to their example.

*A hero ventures forth
from the world of common day
into a region of supernatural wonder:
fabulous forces are there encountered
and a decisive victory is won:
the hero comes back
from this mysterious adventure
with the power to bestow
boons on his fellow man.*[16]

JOSEPH CAMPBELL

*Heroes take journeys,
confront dragons,
and discover the treasure
of their true selves.*[17]

HANNAH SENESH

Firefighters

Over the years, we have often heard New York firefighters referred to as the "Bravest." On September 11 and in the dreadful days of rescue and recovery that followed, they proved themselves true. They charged into a fiery cauldron of peril, raced up hundreds of stairs, and helped save thousands of lives. That's what they do . . . they save lives . . . every day.

Well over three hundred firefighters out of New York City's 9,000 firefighters are missing in what remains of the World Trade Center. The loss is unimaginable: nearly 3 percent of the entire force, including many of the most-experienced commanders. Entire squads disappeared in the smoke and dust.

Ralph Waldo Emerson once said that "man's actions are the picture book of his creeds," and based on what we witnessed, it's time that we consider these men's beliefs.

New Yorker Pat Newman says of firefighters, "They're a different breed. You've been taught to run out of a burning building. They're taught to run in."[18] Even when the walls were cracking and the steel began to weaken, they kept going. And in doing so, many, far too many, of their own ranks fell in the battle.

FIRE CAPTAIN PAT BROWN

Forty-eight years old and a decorated veteran of Vietnam, Fire Captain Pat Brown was one of the most decorated men of the New York Fire Department. He made many rescues during his career that were well documented. Perhaps the most spectacular came in 1991 when he and two of his men rescued panic-stricken victims from a windowsill ledge of an office building. Holding a thick rope in their bare hands and straining and sliding toward the parapet, they lowered two firefighters, one at a time, through billowing black smoke to grab the victims and lower them to safety.

When Brown's company got the call to the World Trade Center and arrived at the north tower, there was no hesitation, even though it was reported that someone yelled, "Don't go in there, Paddy!"

"Are you nuts?" was Brown's only response. "We've got a job to do!"[19]

He and his eleven men rushed up the stairs to take out as many office workers as they could. They perished when the tower collapsed.

The news of Captain Brown came as no surprise to Elissa Wald, the writer of the recently released novel, *Holding Fire*, which was inspired by Brown. "There's nowhere else he'd be but right in the middle of this,"[20] she said. Of her story's character, Captain John Malone, who mirrors Brown's life, she wrote in her book that he is "a legend, not only for the dozens of rescues to his name, but for the insane chances he took all the time. Sometimes after reading the accounts in the medal books, it was hard to believe Malone was alive and walking around."

LADDER 24, ENGINE 1 AND FATHER MYCHAL JUDGE

Who can ever forget the photo of Father Mychal Judge's lifeless body being carried out of the smoke and ruins by his firefighter friends. The sixty-eight-year-old Franciscan priest and chaplain of the New York Fire Department had removed his fire hat while administering the last rites to a firefighter who had been killed by a falling woman's body, and while he prayed he was killed by falling debris. Members of Ladder Co. 24, Engine Co. 1 on West 31st Street, across from St. Francis Church, so loved their priest that they carried his body to nearby St. Peter's Church and then commandeered an ambulance to take the body to their firehouse. "We brought him home," says one firefighter.

Judge, the Brooklyn-born son of Irish immigrants, was remembered as a man "who treated presidents and paupers with the same respect." Firefighter John Slevin says, "He's the guy everybody counted on to get us through the tough times. He always had words that put things in perspective." Last year at a memorial service for the victims of TWA Flight 800, Judge urged his listeners to find strength in their memories of the departed: "Open your hearts, and let their spirit and life keep you going." He was fearless in life and death, and "a saint, a wonderful man," says Mayor Rudy Guiliani.

"We came to bury his voice but not his spirit, his hands but not his works, his heart but not his love," says Michael Duffy, a fellow Franciscan priest and close friend. "Mychal Judge will be on the other side of death to greet [the fallen firefighters]. He'll greet them with that big Irish smile and say, 'Hello, welcome. I want to take you to my Father.' "

Ladder Co. 24, Engine Co. 1 lost seven firefighters in the attack.

ANDREA KAISER

Traveling back to the stationhouse from a training session in Arlington, Virginia, Andrea Kaiser, a thirty-eight-year-old firefighter, looked up as the hijacked American Airlines Flight 77 took dead aim at the Pentagon. The Boeing 757 flew low over her firetruck at top speed and slammed into the Pentagon, a mushroom cloud of smoke billowing upward like an atomic bomb.

Already aware of the other terrorists' attacks in New York, Kaiser gunned her firetruck toward the burning scene and turned on the siren. "No one had to tell me I was in for the fight of my life," she said, arriving among the first wave of firefighters to the scene. "Besides trying to fight a major fire and save lives, I knew there was someone out there trying to kill me."[21] Rushing into the pitch-black inferno, walls crumbled and scorched, she made her way to the third floor, but never found anyone alive, only charred bodies.

BOB BECKWITH

When President Bush arrived at Ground Zero and gave his stirring speech to the rescue workers on September 13, alongside of him stood an older firefighter whom I assumed was in charge of the site. It turns out that he was Bob Beckwith, a sixty-nine-year-old retired firefighter who had volunteered to go into the city and do what he could.

When he was told he should stay home, he was too old,

Beckwith responded, "I couldn't do that. Once a fireman, always a fireman."

His appearance with the President was totally unplanned, and in that moment Bob Beckwith became a patriotic symbol of bravery. Never tell a fireman he's too old!

Firefighter task forces from around the nation joined volunteers such as Bob Beckwith in the recovery effort, but for the New York firefighters the tragedy is consuming. Their search includes finding fellow firefighters, friends, and, in some cases, family members.

To the firefighters of New York, Mayor Rudy Giuliani said, "They took three hundred men or more, but the reality is that we will be strong. We're not going to let them kill our spirits. They just can't."

A Fireman's Prayer

When I am called to duty, God,
Wherever flame may rage,
Give me the strength to save some life,
Whatever be its age.

Help me embrace a little child
Before it is too late,
Or save an older person from
The horror of that fate.

Enable me to be alert
And hear the weakest shout,
And quickly and efficiently
To put the fire out.

I want to fill my calling and
To give the best in me,
To guard my every neighbor
And protect his property.

And if according to my fate,
I am to lose my life,
Please bless with Your protecting hand
My children and my wife.

AUTHOR UNKNOWN

The cost of freedom
is always high—
and Americans
have always paid it.

And one path
we shall never choose,
and that is the path
of surrender or submission.

JOHN F. KENNEDY

OCTOBER 22, 1962, CUBAN MISSILE CRISIS

A TIME TO REMEMBER

Patriotism is heroism—
risking it all
for people
you don't even know.[22]

JONATHAN ALTER

Police

On what was the bloodiest day on American soil since the Civil War, we see why the New York City police are constantly referred to as the "Finest." At a time when hundreds of victims needed saving, they were there. What was said about the character of firemen is every bit as true of the police. When others were in flight from the carnage, we watched the police heroically plunge into the volcano blast and collapsing buildings to rescue victims from the blackness of certain death.

Perhaps the police are best represented by George Howard, an off-duty New York City officer who was one of the first to die at the World Trade Center as he ran to help people escape. As the tower came crashing down, George Howard screamed for other rescue workers to flee, but he stayed to try to save someone. He perished beneath a piece of sheet metal.

During President Bush's speech to Congress on September 20, 2001, he held up Howard's police shield and said, "Some will carry memories of a face and a voice gone forever. And I will carry this. It is my reminder of lives that ended and a task that does not end."

That shield had been given to the President by Howard's mother, Arlene, when he had visited with grieving family members at the Jacob Javits Center in New York. Her son was a Port Authority policeman and father of two sons. He had been one of the first cops on the scene during the 1993 terrorist bombing of the World Trade Center.

"I wanted to give my son's badge to President Bush so history would know what happened here in New York City on this horrible day," Mrs. Howard said. "I wanted my son George and the many like him to be preserved in history and in the memories of generations to come. He loved his work, and he died doing it. There's no greater way to go than the way George died, saving lives."[23]

Over seventy Port Authority police are still missing as I write.

Policeman's Prayer

When I start my tour of duty, God,
Wherever crime may be,
As I walk the darkened streets alone,
Let me be close to thee.

Please give me understanding
With both the young and old.
Let me listen with attention
Until their story's told.

Let me never make a judgment
In a rush or callous way,
But let me hold my patience . . .
Let each man have his say.

Lord, if some dark and dreary night,
I must give my life,
Lord, with your everlasting love
protect my children and my wife.

AUTHOR UNKNOWN

*Heroism
is to stand held
only by the invisible chain
of higher duty,
and, so standing,
to let the fire creep up
to the heart.*

PHILLIP BROOKS

A TIME TO ACT

*You feel like you should
be asking them
[the firefighters and rescue workers]
for their autographs.
They are the heroes.*[24]

DEREK JETER

Good Samaritans

The stories are endless. Construction workers, doctors, nurses, paramedics, and others from all walks of life who rushed to the scene and immediately performed whatever services they could render. In suburbs around New York, residents set up phone chains to ensure that schoolchildren whose parents might have both been in the city had a place to stay until they made their way home, if they made it home.

Medical-supply companies poured in supplies without being asked and at no cost. Some came to comfort the grieving, and others to provide food for those laboring around the clock. In cities all over the United States, the Red Cross reported blood centers filled as people eagerly donated blood.

The people who follow represent the thousands of Good Samaritans who gave of their lives during the events of September 11.

SOLDIERS

In the explosion and chaos inside the Pentagon, one secretary was in shock and couldn't move. A young soldier hoisted her on his back and carried her across a wall to safety. "You never leave somebody behind," said Colonel Mark Perrin, the senior officer on the scene. "Nobody was out to save themselves first."[25]

MEDICAL PERSONNEL

When officials at Washington Hospital Center started to run low on human tissue for burn victims from the Pentagon attack, a group of men from a Dallas hospital piled into a car with an ice chest containing human skin and drove overnight to Washington because air traffic had been halted.

OFFICE WORKERS

Consider Michael Benfante, thirty-six, and John Cerqueira, twenty-two, who were working on the eighty-first floor of the north tower at the World Trade Center when the first plane hit just eight floors above them.[26] As they made their descent down the stairs to the sixty-eighth floor, they came upon a woman stranded in a wheelchair. In an agonizing hour-long battle, fighting blinding smoke and exhausted muscles, the two men carried the disabled woman in a special chair kept in the stairwell for such emergencies. Finally reaching the street, they got her safely away in an emergency van when the tower collapsed. Running again for their lives, the two men dove under a truck and barely escaped death.

EMTS

Michelle March, a twenty-nine-year-old emergency medical technician, was among the first EMTs to arrive at the south tower. But when the tower collapsed, all she could do was run for her life. "I noticed that the debris was picking people up and slamming them into buildings. So I grabbed a pole and held on for dear life." As debris struck her, she said, "I told God, 'I'm not dying today,' so I held on no matter how many bricks were hitting me. I felt ash go down my throat, so I made myself vomit because it was asphyxiating. My head was hurting from the hits, but I refused to lose consciousness."[27] And she made it through and spent one night in the hospital. One of the other EMTs whom she works with died, and another was missing.

ARCHITECTS

Ronnie Clifford, a forty-seven-year-old Irish architect was in the lobby of the Marriott Hotel after the first plane hit. The Marriot sits between, as well as directly below, the Twin Towers. Seeing a charred woman, her fingernails melting off and clothes burned on her skin, Clifford sheltered her with his coat and protected her when the second plane hit. He took her name and medical details, then helped get her to the nearest ambulance. Later he learned that his sister and niece and their close family friend had been passengers in the separate planes that crashed into the towers.

NATIONAL SECURITY EXPERTS

John O'Neill retired from the FBI in August and was known as America's pit bull on terrorism. He was the head of the bureau's national-security operations in New York City and oversaw the on-site investigations in the 1998 embassy bombings in Kenya and Tanzania and the 2000 attack on the U.S.S. *Cole* in Yemen, both thought to be the work of groups linked to Osama bin Laden. At forty-nine, O'Neill had taken the job of chief of security at the World Trade Center just two days before the terrorists attacked.

After the first strike on the Trade Center, O'Neill is thought to have evacuated his office on the thirty-fourth floor of the north tower. He made a few calls from the street—including one to his son to let him know he was unharmed and one to FBI headquarters. Then he went back to help with the rescue effort. He has not been seen since.

PARAMEDICS

Mike Cahill, a paramedic for the Alexandria, Virginia, fire department, was driving near the Pentagon, listening to a radio report about the World Trade Center attack, when he saw a huge column of smoke rise above the trees in front of him. Rushing to the scene, he pulled out his first-aid bag and ran toward the flaming building. Everyone he saw coming toward him was burned, and "some of these guys still literally had smoke or steam coming off of their body or skin."[28] He helped dozens of victims, cutting off melted clothing and dousing them with saline solution before getting them to a nearby lawn while more explosions rocked the crash scene.

THE INVISIBLE ONES

Then there are the heroes we don't see. The ones who search the rubble for body parts, no matter how small, and bag them carefully. The ones who will match the pieces with victims and bring a small degree of closure to grieving families. The ones who will take care of the burn victims through weeks and weeks of recovery. And on and on it goes.

With so many fatalities and injuries, the circle of Good Samaritans is beyond description.

*Part of the magic
of heroes and heroines
has always been their ability
to embody a vision of life
that at the moment
is not yet developed enough....*

*Heroes are not always
just reflections
of what has already happened
but are also harbingers
of what is to come.*[29]

TODD BRENNAN

A TIME TO ENDURE

*The boy stood
on the burning deck.*

*When all but he
had fled.*[30]

FELICIA HEMANS

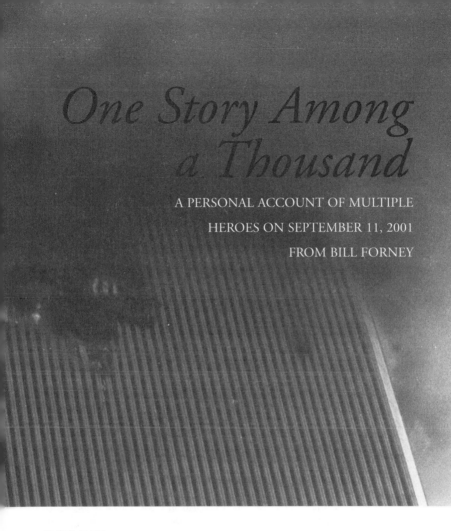

One Story Among a Thousand

A PERSONAL ACCOUNT OF MULTIPLE
HEROES ON SEPTEMBER 11, 2001
FROM BILL FORNEY

8:00 A.M.: I arrive at the World Trade Center complex and stop at the bank in the tunnels below the south tower to make a deposit at the ATM.

8:15 A.M.: I get to the eighty-fifth floor of the north World Trade Center tower, where my company, SMW Trading, has its offices. I begin preparing reports for another day of trading at the New York Mercantile Exchange, located in a separate building five minutes away from our office.

8:43 A.M.: I am busy with the reports, sitting at the table in the center of the office with my back to the outside windows. Out of the corner of my eye, I notice my boss suddenly moving quickly out of his office. Then, without warning, there is a horrific explosion that rocks our office, followed immediately by a change in the air pressure and a ghostly blast of air shooting like a cannon through the office. I feel myself being tossed from my chair and onto the floor as the front door slams shut and papers are whipped into the air around me.

Lying on the floor, my first thought is that we're going to die. I feel the tower shaking furiously, lurching back and forth with a sickening vengeance for what seems to last five or ten seconds. Every nerve inside of me is screaming that the building is going to topple or crumble . . . but finally it stops. And the building is still standing.

As I get to my feet, I look around the office in disbelief. Everyone is staring numbly at one another, no idea of what happened or what to say.

"Was it a bomb?" someone asks.

"No," our boss says, pointing toward his office. "It was a plane. I saw it barely miss the Empire State Building and come straight for our building."

I immediately move toward the front door, but someone yells to not open it. The hallway is on fire. Rob "Opie" Leder, one of my co-workers, and I touch the door and find it's cool. Slowly, I open the door and peer into the pitch black smoke in the hallway. The smell is horrible, unlike any smoke I've ever smelled. It smells of metal, of jet fuel, of rancid concrete, and things unspeakable.

Overwhelmed by it all, I close the door and look back around the office. Everyone is too shocked and confused to move.

Opie was the first to say it. "I gotta get outta here!"

"I'm with you, man," I heard myself saying.

I open the door again, and the smoke is thinner. Down the hallway I see the orange glow of a fire smoldering around the corner. I can hear the muffled sounds of some guys yelling for help from another office, but they're too afraid to open their door.

Before we leave, I grab the black SMW jacket I wear to the trading floor and put it on. It's full of pick cards, order tickets, my empty water bottle, a calculator, a pen, cough drops and gum, and trading analyzers. Then I fill my water bottle, while Opie waits at the door, ready to bolt. Almost everyone in the office wants to evacuate.

"Where's Marvin? Did he leave?" someone calls out.

"Maybe he's in the bathroom," a voice responds.

"I'll check it," I said, stepping into the hallway and inhaling the noxious stench. Behind me my co-workers are following. To the left is another hallway with three small fires burning, debris everywhere, and the lights are out. In front of me is an office with a man peeking out and several terrified people behind him. To the right is another hallway, the bathroom, and the stairwell.

I pull open the bathroom door, and everything is in pristine condition, as though nothing has happened. I call out for Marvin, but there's no answer. So we head down to the stairs.

We move quickly down the stairs, and there are few people in the stairwell yet. At the eighty-first floor, Opie stops to help another guy break out some fire extinguishers, and we each grab one. But when we get to the seventy-second level, people are coming back up the stairs.

"What's wrong?" someone calls out.

"There's a door pinned shut below," the answer sounds. "Try that floor."

We walk out into the hall to find another stairwell. There's a lot of damage here. Wires and debris are scattered everywhere. Fires are smoldering in the rubble, and an entire wall has blown down in the hallway. I cover my face and try not to look, fearing another explosion. We find another stairwell at the other end of the hall.

There are a lot more people on these stairs, and the descent slows. We try to use Opie's cell phone, but it's impossible to get a connection. The display glares out: "Service unavailable at this time."

At about the sixty-fifth floor, Opie is still trying to use the cell phone, but the service remains down. We stop on a large platform, and I notice a woman rocking back and forth directly behind me. She is barefoot, holding her shoes, and asks me for a swig of water. She uses the water to wet her shirt and cover her mouth against the sickening stench.

"I have two children," she says anxiously but politely. "I have to get out of here."

We start moving again, and the woman makes good progress. She passes people where she can but is getting frantic.

At the sixtieth floor, the cell phones are still not working. I toss my investor's business daily that I've been carrying—not exactly important stuff at the moment. I think to myself that I'm trashing the building, which makes me feel bad.

On the fiftieth there's a man walking down the stairs with blood covering half of his face and a bandage on his head. Others pass him, and he's in obvious pain. Everyone is calm, orderly, and supportive. Nobody takes advantage of the path. No one pushes ahead. Such calm, such unselfishness in the face of tragedy. You can feel the quiet adrenaline surging.

There are rumors of a second plane. Some people are making jokes to ease the strain.

We have carried the fire extinguishers all the way to the forty-ninth floor. I'm still wearing my jacket, sweating like crazy, and my shirt is untucked and unbuttoned.

At the forty-fifth, still no cell phones will work. We meet a firefighter heading up the stairs. He's a reassuring presence, giving words of encouragement. At thirty-five, there are more firefighters with serious equipment in their hands and on their backs. At thirty, the door to that floor is open, where firefighters have set up base camp. They've dropped their gear and are tending some injured people. All the floors below have been secured, and they're working their way up, trying to save the people who remain above us.

At twenty-five, a man with a cane struggles down the stairs, and another man is helping him. When we pass them, our descent starts moving faster and the stops lessen. Maybe he was the bottleneck.

At twenty, a woman named Juliette is struggling to get down. She is exhausted and laboring for breath. Opie and I offer water and help, which she accepts. We give her a few seconds to rest, then Opie takes her heavy purse and coat. He walks in front of her, and I go behind. We tell people to pass us on our left.

Floor fifteen, then ten, and then five. At two, I can see light—outside light. We're close to being home free, which spurs us on. We finally exit the stairwell, go into the lobby at street level, facing east toward a courtyard I don't really recognize. It must be in the middle of the World Trade Center complex.

In the courtyard, I recognize colors. Green from a small tree, gray from buildings. Blue sky, somewhere. Black, too. Black stuff on the green and the ground, small puffs of smoke. It must be debris from wreckage. What looks like a person's leg. I can't focus . . . my mind is wandering. I don't want to look.

Firefighters lead us to the escalators, which are not working. There's so much debris on them that we have to climb over. We go down slowly with Juliette. A few people complain that we're walking too slowly.

"What if you needed help?" I ask, which keeps them quiet.

We get down to the lower level, to the glass doors separating the north tower from the shops that are underground at the World Trade Center. All the glass is completely blasted out. It's eerie down here. The sprinklers are on, and people are worried about their clothes. The shops are deserted, but some of the lights are still on. Water is collecting in puddles, and ceiling tiles have fallen here and there. This usually noisy, bustling underground is virtually silent.

"Keep moving!" orders one of the firefighters.

We pass some shops and the entrance to the south tower. The firefighters lead us northeast, around a corner. We stop, and Juliette needs to rest, but the firefighters urge us on.

"Could I have some water?" asks Juliette.

Just then, I hear a faint noise behind us that sounds like rumbling water. No, it's people . . . screaming people who are running furiously, a tidal wave before the crescendo. What are they running from?

"Run!" someone cries.

We start running, but part of the underground goes black, as though someone flicked the off-switch. We take three or four steps, then Opie slips and falls sideways. People yell for us to get down, and we dive to the ground.

The blast feels like a hurricane passing. I grope for a small corner and ball up as fast as I can. Covering my head with both arms, I grimace, mouth open, teeth clenched. For the second time in an hour, I am sure I'm going to die. Something is pelting me: shards of glass, pieces of debris. I wait for something big to sever me in two, and then the chaos subsides. (Much later, I found out this was the south Twin Tower coming down.)

I open my eyes. I've gone blind. Nothing but black. Maybe I didn't open my eyes. I close them tight, then open them again. Nothingness. I take a breath and inhale metal, ash, and concrete. I cough, then breathe again. More ash. With each breath I take, it's more painful.

"Opie! Juliette!" I gasp.

I hear Juliette, but no response from Opie.

"Opie!" I repeat, then repeat again.

Finally, I hear his cough and a faint response. He's alive, and so is Juliette. A few seconds pass, then somebody steps on me.

"What's that down there?" someone asks in the darkness.

"A person, dude," I say.

"Oh, sorry," the voice responds.

I gather my wits, now that I've been stepped on, and see a glimmer of light from behind. A fireman's floodlight. It's nearly impossible to see anything. The air is thick with dust and ash. I can see silhouettes of people now. I see the man who stepped on me. I see things blown all around us. I stand up carefully. Opie is hunched over on the ground, coughing up some stuff and spitting it out. He stands up slowly.

The fireman starts to walk past, and others are following. I pull Juliette to her feet. We can't let the fireman get away with his light. I grab Opie's hand, and the group of us form a human chain. We follow the fireman, knowing that without his light we'd be crawling, and it would take forever to get out.

"Bill, is that you?" a raspy voice calls out.

It's Jonathan, one of our firm's partners who had come in from Chicago. He joins our group, and we trudge slowly on for about eighty yards. Then we see natural light again and walk toward it. It's upstairs, the street level. There's another escalator with more debris on it. We walk up it and get to the top, where the glass doors are shattered and a big rug is blocking the entrance, but only slightly. We make our way carefully over the rug, and we're outside.

It looks like a war zone—a monochromatic gray landscape covered in dirt and ash. We're in a movie, an abandoned city. The visibility is fifty feet at most, but I never once look up. I'm still holding on to Juliette, and I feel as though I'm pulling her too much, so I slow down. The soot on the ground is several inches thick, and the air is full of dust and ash.

"Just keep walking," I say to Juliette. "Don't stop. We need to keep walking. Where's Opie?"

"He's in front of us," she whispers.

I know, but I can't see him.

We reach a street, at least I think it's a street. It's so covered in ash, probably four inches deep, I can't believe it. We keep walking across the street. Somebody is running toward us, shouting to look for bodies under cars. I glance around for bodies but don't see any.

We walk past a church with a graveyard and stop. I cough up the ash in my mouth and lungs, take a mouthful of water, and spit out blackness. I tell Juliette to do the same.

"Where's my purse and coat?" she asks.

"I don't know," I answer. "Opie had them. Where is he?"

I call out for Opie, and then see him up ahead. We start walking again and get to another street. There's less ash here and the air is better.

"I need my purse," says Juliette. "I have no money. What will I do?"

"Don't worry," I reassure her. "I'll give you some money. You're alive. Be happy you're alive."

We meet up with Opie and come to a man who's standing in a store doorway. He opens the door and tells us to come in. Juliette is exhausted and wants to stay there, sitting down on some stairs. Opie and I want to keep moving. We each give her $10 to get home, exchange phones numbers, then kiss her on the forehead and wish her good luck.

Opie and I walk about ten minutes. People have lined the sidewalks, looking at the north tower that is still burning. We keep walking away. Then a horrifying gasp, and people begin crying. We turn around as the north tower collapses. Our building. We watch it go down, floor by floor by floor.

It's beyond comprehension. We turn around and keep walking, eventually meeting three co-workers.

"Thank God, you're alive," they say. And we concur.

We keep walking, just trying to get away, trying to find a pay phone that doesn't have lines twenty people deep. We want to call somebody and tell them we're alive. We walk about thirty minutes, then find a corner store that has a pay phone that's not being used. We take turns and call our wives, our parents, and our friends. We're okay, we say, we're alive.

We all walk home together. I walk the entire length of Manhattan to get home to the upper west side. On the way, I stop and see my sister and some friends. I am not alone. Hundreds of other New Yorkers are walking home. It's all too surreal.

WEDNESDAY, SEPTEMBER 12, 2001
9:00 A.M.: I receive a call from Opie. Everyone made it out of our office. Marvin is alive.

MONDAY, SEPTEMBER 16, 2001
2:01 P.M.: I receive a letter from my bank. The ATM deposit went through.

*It is now the moment
when by common consent
we pause to become conscious
of our national life
and to rejoice in it,
to recall what our country
has done for each of us,
and to ask ourselves
what we can do
for our country in return.*

OLIVER WENDELL HOLMES, JR.

MEMORIAL DAY ADDRESS

MAY 30, 1884

And so, my fellow Americans:
ask not what your country can do for you—
ask what you can do for your country.

My fellow citizens of the world:
ask not what America can do for you,
but what together we can do
for the freedom of the world.

JOHN F. KENNEDY
PRESIDENTIAL INAUGURAL ADDRESS
JANUARY 20, 1961

How Then Shall We Live?

As I write this, thousands upon thousands of tons of what once was the World Trade Center are being sifted for the remains of an estimated 6,000 human beings. At that lonely field in Pennsylvania, archeologists sift the ground slowly and patiently for any possible remains of the heroes of United Flight 93. The embattled section of the Pentagon still entombs the bodies of many precious souls who were deeply loved and grieved.

The indiscriminate slaughter of civilians encompassed at least sixty-seven countries. Britain lost over two hundred fifty people. That is more than all those killed in England itself in decades of Irish Republican Army terror attacks. India is missing about two hundred fifty people, and Germany one hundred seventy.

We watched the same unbelievable television images over and over again, trying and failing to fathom the massive, heinous murder perpetrated on our own soil. America . . . we the people and what the nation stands for . . . were under attack. Not just under attack, but "at war," President Bush declared. "There has been an act of war declared upon America by terrorists, and we will respond accordingly."

Two full generations of Americans have grown up who have not faced such a challenge.

With the fall of the Berlin Wall on November 9, 1989, which represented the final chapter of the Cold War years, capitalism was embraced across the world, and the notion of the "enemies of capitalism" seemed to drift away. Living in peace and affluence, we were lulled into the stupor of American indifference and self-contentment.

We closed our eyes and plugged our ears when we were warned that the day would come when terrorists would strike out at us on a monumental scale. The world out there no longer seemed a significant threat to our welfare. Our biggest concern was the economy, the size of our houses, and how comfortably we might retire.

September 11, 2001 ended all that.

It only took a few minutes on a Tuesday morning to burst the bubble of our national illusion toward invulnerability. Lives were shattered as quickly as buildings shattered. Economics and politics changed in a moment. Foreign policy and national security and civil liberties were altered without notice.

Stunned with horror that quickly found its way to anger, we have heard the call to war against an enemy that cannot be easily identified. The unavoidable question looms before us: Will we have the resolve to defeat this enemy that threatens the freedom of every one of us?

In President Bush's speech at a prayer service in the National Cathedral in Washington, he gave us this challenge: "In every generation, the world has produced enemies of human freedom. They have attacked America because we are freedom's home and defender, and the commitment of our fathers is now the call of our times."

How then shall we live?

The headline in Sebastian Mallaby's article in the *Washington*

Post points us in the right direction: "Thatcher's reply to IRA terror: 'Life must go on.' "[31] In the very early hours of October 12, 1984, an IRA bomb exploded in the Grand Hotel in Brighton, England, where most of the British cabinet was staying. The blast blew out the windows in the suite where Prime Minister Margaret Thatcher was staying, and the bathroom where she had been in two minutes earlier was demolished. Four stories of rooms collapsed upon each other, killing four and injuring more than thirty.

Within one hour's time, the "Iron Lady" stepped before the television cameras and declared, "Life must go on." Later that morning, she marched through the front entrance of the Conservative Party conference, defying the police's advice to enter through the back door, and pronounced, "All attempts to destroy democracy by terrorism will fail. It must be business as usual." She would not cower in fear, she would not change her agenda, and she insisted by her example that right would triumph over evil.

We may never look at another jet in the sky in the same casual way, we may cringe inside when we hear a siren wail, we may think twice about going into a tall building or purchasing an airline ticket. But we can never allow our enemies to hold us hostage with fear. We can never adopt a policy of helplessness—personally or nationally. "Life must go on," even when we are at war.

Winston Churchill, who in the dark days of the Battle of Britain mobilized his people with "blood, toil, tears, and sweat" to meet its "finest hour," said, "There are many things worse than war. Slavery is worse than war. Dishonor is worse than war." And living under the fear of terrorism is worse than war.

Historians recall that during the Civil War, Abraham Lincoln insisted that the construction of the nation's Capitol dome be completed. Soon after the bombing of Pearl Harbor, a list of security measures at the White House were placed before President Franklin Roosevelt: mounting machine guns on the roof, camouflaging the building, covering the skylights. Roosevelt said no to most of the recommendations. The message from Lincoln and Roosevelt was clear: America was not afraid. America would come through the battle.

As our nation rises up to defend our freedom, so too must we rise up to support her and our leaders and the men and women who will fight for us. Both require our utmost backing. General Norman Schwarzkopf said, "It doesn't take a hero to order men into battle. It takes a hero to be one of those who goes into battle."

The terrorists will not go away. They are ruthless warriors who slaughter innocents and reign through terror and anarchy. War and destruction are their way of life. There radical faith is simply a cover for who they really are.

In Palestine a children's song is played on TV: "How pleasant is the smell of martyrs . . . the land enriched by the blood, the blood pouring out of a fresh body." How many young people have already embraced that message?

The suicidal bombers have a phrase, *Bassamat al-farah*, the smile of joy. They are taught that they are guaranteed immediate admission to paradise, where seventy-two black-eyed virgins await their pleasure. Theirs is a covenant of death.

In 1998, Osama bin Laden proclaimed it a religious duty "to kill the Americans and their allies, civilian and military, in any country in which it is possible to do it." The message could not have been clearer to his network of assassins, or to us.

"Terrorism by Islamic extremists represents the biggest threat to the free world. The aim of this terrorism is to destroy the foundations of democratic society and Westerners," said the Israeli Defense Minister, Binyamin Ben Eliezer. And the weapons they bring next time . . . and the next time . . . will be far more sophisticated than commercial jets loaded with fuel.

British Prime Minister Tony Blair says concerning the terrorists: "They have no moral inhibition on the slaughter of the innocent. If they could have murdered not 7,000 but 70,000, does anyone doubt they would have done so and rejoiced in it? There is no compromise possible with such people, no meeting of minds, no point of understanding with such terror. There is just a choice: Defeat it or be defeated by it, and defeat it we must."

"One sword keeps another in its sheath," wrote George Herbert in 1640. That wisdom appears to no longer apply. Terrorists must be separated from their sheaths.

The terrorists do not and will not fear us. We must not fear them. This is our land and way of life that we defend. We are targeted for death—our families, our friends, our neighbors. In a single moment we learned that innocence protects no one from blind fanaticism.

With the safety and liberty of our country at stake, the only real question is, "What can I do to help?"

[Heroism is]
when honor
seems to compromise
with death.

ROBERT G. INGERSOLL

A TIME TO MOURN

Our doubts are traitors,
and make us lose
the good we oft might win
by fearing the attempt.

SHAKESPEARE

We Dare Not Back Down

John F. Kennedy warned us long ago: "There are risks and costs to a program of action—but they are far less than the long-range risks and costs of comfortable inaction."

Our President and national leaders have incredibly difficult decisions to make in our behalf. No one has hinted that the road ahead will be easy or without sacrifice. But it is time that we get behind our leaders and dedicate ourselves to whatever course of action is required to bring victory.

With the victims and injured of September 11 fresh in our national consciousness, may we never dismiss the danger of terrorism again, or the blessings of living in a prosperous, democratic nation.

If we back down in fear, we need to prepare ourselves for family members standing in lines for hours to scan lists of victims, looking for a familiar name, then filling out forms describing the missing person in detail and providing DNA samples.

We will see more walls plastered full with pictures of missing men and women and children of all ages, shapes, sizes, and backgrounds, holding their loved ones in their arms, wrestling with their kids, or relaxing on vacation. Smiling faces of the presumed dead beckon our tears and prayers.

We need to ready ourselves for cruise missiles and more aircraft, nuclear devices, attacks on agriculture and water systems, chemical and biological weapons, and cyberterrorism. Terrorists will use whatever means available to strike, with a goal for maximizing the death count.

There will be more medical teams that perform triage on street-corners. Color coding will become familiar to us all: black for dead, red for immediately life-threatening wounds, yellow for serious, non-life-threatening, and green for the walking wounded.

We need to prepare ourselves for repeated scenes of terrified people leaping to their deaths from burning offices and where cadaver-sniffing dogs become useless, overwhelmed by the pervasive stench of death.

Get ready for more of the wounded little voices of children, broken and choked with grief over the loss of parents.

We need to be prepared for unlimited numbers of stories such as Candy Glazer, whose husband, Edmund, was killed in the American Airlines Flight 11.

"Honey," she said to her four-year-old son, pierced with indescribable grief. "Daddy's been in an accident."

Nathan looked at her. "What do you mean?"

"Daddy's dead."

The boy started sobbing and asked, "Can't we fix him?"

I, for one, don't want to make those preparations. We need to walk through our fears, win back our freedom, and re-create our world into a safe place worthy of the heroes who have gone before us. We cannot close our doors to the world and free trade, despite it always being a door that makes us vulnerable to some degree.

In the words of Todd Beamer, our hero from Flight 93, we must have the resolve of will to take our stand and say,

"Let's roll!"

There are stars whose radiance
is visible on earth
though they have long been extinct.

There are people whose brilliance
continues to light the world
though they are no longer among the living.

These lights are particularly bright
when the night is dark.

They light the way
for Mankind.[32]

HANNAH SENESH

Now fear the LORD
and serve him with all faithfulness.

Throw away the gods your forefathers
worshiped beyond the River and in Egypt,
and serve the LORD.

But if serving the LORD
seems undesirable to you,
then choose for yourselves this day
whom you will serve,
whether the gods your forefathers
served beyond the River,
or the gods of the Amorites,
in whose land you are living.

But as for me
and my household,
we will serve the LORD.

JOSHUA 24:14-15

A TIME TO RISE UP

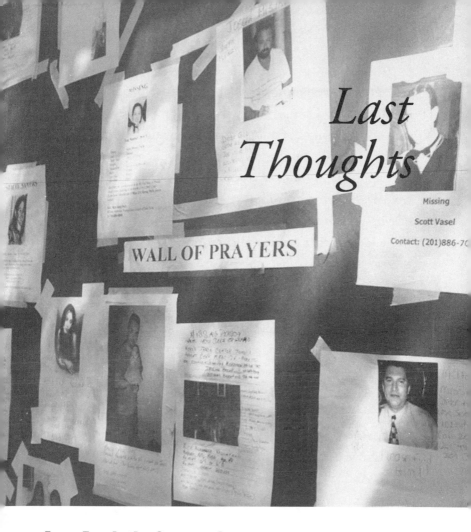

Last Thoughts

Missing

Scott Vasel

Contact: (201)886-7(

WALL OF PRAYERS

Anne Frank, the German-born Jewish teenager who perished in a Nazi concentration camp in 1945, kept a diary during her years in hiding while the Germans occupied the Netherlands. Her bravery in the face of prolonged terror has been a rich source of inspiration for the entire world. She wrote these incredible words:

"In spite of everything, I still believe that people are really good at heart. I simply can't build up my hopes on a foundation consisting of confusion, misery, and death. I see the world gradually being turned into a wilderness, I hear the ever-approaching thunder, which will destroy us, too, I can feel the suffering of millions, and yet, if I look up into the heavens, I think that it will all come right, that this cruelty will end, and that peace and tranquility will return again. In the meantime, I must uphold my ideals, for perhaps the time will come when I shall be able to carry them out."[33]

We have seen the wilderness and heard the thunder. Now is our time to look up into the heavens and consider what shall be.

In the days that followed September 11, as a collective nation we heard countless stories of the lives and the deaths of our fellow Americans. Every life is a story, and every photo made us wish we could have known these people. Every life is precious. And we it owe it to them to treasure their memory and live our lives accordingly.

Brian Sweeney, a thirty-eight-year-old passenger on United Flight 175, left these final words to his wife on the answering machine. "Hi, Jules. It's Brian. I'm on a plane that's been hijacked. It doesn't look good. I just want to tell you that I love you. I hope that I call you again. But if not, I want you to have fun. I want you to live your life. I know I'll see you someday."

Flight 175 crashed through the south face of the south World Trade Center tower, but Brian Sweeney's last moments with his wife will live on for a lifetime. He gave her his undying love. He gave her the freedom to move forward with her life, even if he was gone. And he gave her hope that the day will come when they will see each other again. No one will ever be able to take that away from her.

A husband kisses his wife good-bye in the morning, not knowing it's truly good-bye.

We give hugs, not realizing that tomorrow does not always come.

We hear our loved one's voice, unaware that it may be the last time.

We hold a cherished hand, not realizing that life is about to change dramatically . . . sometimes forever.

Patricia Coombs dropped her husband, Jeffrey, off at the train station for a four-day business trip. He was one of the ninety-two people who boarded American Airlines Flight 11. As they parted, Patricia recalled, "For some odd reason, as he was walking to the train, it went through my mind very quickly that that was a casual kiss. What if that was it? I don't know why I thought it. It was just a quick, fleeting thought."[34]

Most of us do not live with the sense of awareness that sixty-three-year-old Ray Downey did. He was New York City's fire chief of special operations and most decorated firefighter. Downey headed the search and rescue efforts at the World Trade Center bombing in 1993, the Oklahoma City bombing in 1995, and the TWA Flight 800 explosion in 1996. He spoke these words at another firefighter's funeral less than two weeks before he disappeared when the second World Trade Center tower collapsed: "We have to accept this as part of the job. Sometimes in this job, good-bye really is good-bye."[35]

Yet "good-bye really is good-bye" can be true for any of us, and what a difference it makes if we are prepared at that moment. Lyzbeth Glick said that in their last phone conversation, she and Jeremy said "I love you" a thousand times. Amazingly, she can now say from her heart: "I don't feel like there were things left undone with my relationship with Jeremy. We did it all, and I don't feel like I've left anything unsaid to him, and I don't feel like he's left anything unsaid to me. And I don't think many people who are so young can say that."

I'm not certain that many people at any age can say that, but the possibility is as open to us as it was to the Glicks.

And even beyond that, there's more for us to consider about how we live our daily lives. When we're gone, what will remain? Consider these extraordinary words of Lisa Beamer as she spoke of her husband: "Todd was a man of faith. He knew this life was not all there is, and this life was just to prepare him for his eternity with God and Jesus. Every day he made sure he lived his life in a way that was pleasing to God and that would help him know God better, and he always acted on that right to the end."[36]

"Some people live their whole lives, long lives, without having left anything behind," Lisa continued. "My sons will be told their whole lives that their father was a hero, that he saved lives. It's a great legacy for a father to leave his children."

The legacy of Todd Beamer came far too early in life, but in a moment's notice he rose up, and the convictions of his life became a national treasure.

It's not too late to rewrite your life story.

It's not too late to leave behind a legacy of love.

It's not too late to ask God to give you a glimpse of His love for the people in your life and how He values them.

It's not too late to start living with the awareness that every minute counts, that personal character counts, and that you can make a difference in the world.

I offer you the Bible as your starting point. I can assure you that inside its pages you will discover several generations of people who faced the same issues we face in our world today. You will see the rise and fall of kingdoms and powers. You will find comfort and strength in a personal God who loves us and gave His own Son to redeem us from the evil in our own hearts. And you will read of a coming time when God himself will wipe away every tear from our eyes, death will be destroyed, and sickness and pain and sorrow will be no more.

If you want to live in joy and peace, whether in life or death, why not go to the Source?

Peace I leave with you;
my peace I give you.

I do not give to you
as the world gives.

Do not let your hearts be troubled
and do not be afraid.

JESUS CHRIST
JOHN 14:27

Psalm 46

God is our refuge and strength,
an ever-present help in trouble.

Therefore we will not fear, though the earth give way
and the mountains fall into the heart of the sea,
though its waters roar and foam
and the mountains quake with their surging.

There is a river whose streams make glad the city of God,
the holy place where the Most High dwells.

God is within her, she will not fall;
God will help her at break of day.

Nations are in uproar, kingdoms fall;
he lifts his voice, the earth melts.

The LORD Almighty is with us;

the God of Jacob is our fortress.

Come and see the works of the LORD,
the desolations he has brought on the earth.

He makes wars cease to the ends of the earth;

he breaks the bow and shatters the spear,
he burns the shields with fire.

"Be still, and know that I am God;
I will be exalted among the nations,
I will be exalted in the earth."

The LORD Almighty is with us;
the God of Jacob is our fortress.

A TIME FOR FAITH

There is no security on this earth.

Only opportunity.

DOUGLAS MACARTHUR

How Firm a Foundation

A PORTION OF
DR. BILLY GRAHAM'S
MESSAGE FROM FRIDAY,
SEPTEMBER 14, 2001,
AT THE NATIONAL CATHEDRAL
IN WASHINGTON, D.C.

We've always needed God from the very beginning of this nation, but today we need Him especially. The Bible's words are our hope: "God is our refuge and strength, an ever-present help in trouble. Therefore we will not fear, though the earth give way and the mountains fall into the heart of the sea" (Psalm 46:1-2).

But why does God allow evil like this to take place? Perhaps that is what you are asking. You may even be angry at God. I want to assure you that God understands those feelings. And God can be trusted, even when life seems at its darkest.

I have been asked hundreds of times why God allows tragedy and suffering. I have to confess that I really do not know the answer totally, even to my own satisfaction. I have to accept, by faith, that God is sovereign, and He is a God of love and mercy and compassion in the midst of suffering.

None of us will ever forget the pictures of our courageous firefighters and police, or the hundreds standing patiently in line to donate blood. A tragedy like this could have torn this country apart, but instead it has united us and we have become a family.

We never know when we, too, will be called into eternity. I doubt if even one of those people who got on those planes, or walked into the World Trade Center, or the Pentagon that morning thought it would be the last day of their lives. And that's why each of us needs to face our own spiritual need and commit ourselves to God and His will now.

Yes, our nation has been attacked, buildings destroyed, and lives lost. But now we have a choice: whether to implode and disintegrate emotionally and spiritually as a people and a nation, or to rebuild on a solid foundation. I believe we are in the process of starting to rebuild. That foundation is our trust in God.

My prayer today is that we will feel the loving arms of God wrapped around us, and will know in our hearts that He will never forsake us as we trust in Him.

HOW YOU CAN HELP

Here is a list of organizations accepting contributions for relief efforts and bereaved families:

American Red Cross: Contribute to the National Disaster Relief Fund by calling 800-435-7669 (800-257-7575 in Spanish). Find your local chapter or more information at www.redcross.org.

United Way: The United Way of New York and the New York Community Trust have created a fund specifically for victims and their families. Mail your check or money order to United Way of New York City, 2 Park Avenue, New York, N.Y. 10016. Or call 800-710-8002. Go to www.uwnyc.org.

Salvation Army: Mail your check to Salvation Army, P.O. Box C635, West Nyack, N.Y. 10994-1739. Write either "Twin Towers Relief" or "Pentagon Relief" on the memo line to earmark your donation. To use your MasterCard or Visa, call 800-SAL-ARMY (800-725-2769).

America's Second Harvest: Through local affiliates, this charity is supplying relief workers and shelters with food and water. Call 800-344-8070.

Mercy Corps: Supporting local agencies to help provide trauma counseling, especially for children. Call 800-852-2100 or mail checks to Mercy Corps, Dept. W., U.S. Emergency Fund, P.O. Box 2669, Portland, Ore. 97208. Donate online at www.mercycorps.org.

New York City Firefighters 9-11 Disaster Relief Fund: Mail checks to Firehouse.com, 9658 Baltimore Avenue, Suite 350, College Park, Md. 20740. All money will be used for families of deceased firefighters.

New York Police & Fire Widow's and Children's Benefit Fund: Mail checks to New York Police & Fire Widow's and Children's Benefit Fund, P.O. Box 3713, Grand Central Station, New York, N.Y. 10163. Or visit their website at www.nypfwc.org.

ENDNOTES

1. Henry Kissinger, "With Faint Praise," *New York Times Book Review*, 16 July 1995.

2. Sidney Hook, *The Hero in History* (Piscataway, N.J.: Transaction Publishers, 1992 reprint edition), p. 9.

3. Nathan Hale, last words attributed to him before being hanged by the British as a spy during the Revolutionary War, 22 September 1776.

4. *Star*, 2 October 2001, p. 9.

5. Arthur Ashe, "Points to Ponder," *Reader's Digest*, August 1994.

6. *Dateline NBC*, Maria Shriver interview, "A Likely Hero," 23 September 2001.

7. *Star Tribune* (Minneapolis), 19 September 2001.

8. Ibid.

9. Ronald Steel, opening words, "Will He or Won't He?" *New York Times Book Review*, 17 September 1995.

10. Sidney Hook, ibid.

11. Daniel J. Boorsten, quoted in Ponchittta Pierce, "Who Are Our Heroes?" *Parade Magazine*, 6 August 1995.

12. In George F. Kennan, letter to Henry Munroe Rogers, 25 July 1921.

13. Henry Fairly, "Too Rich for Heroes," *Harper's*, November 1978.

14. Kitty Kelley, "An 80-Year Hitting Streak," *New York Times*, 25 February 1995.

15. Arthur M. Schlesinger, Jr., *A Thousand Days: John F.*

Kennedy in the White House (Boston: Houghton Mifflin Company, 1965), 4.9.

16. Joseph Campbell, *The Hero's Journey* (Shaftesbury, Dorset: Element Books Limited, 1999), xv.

17. Hannah Senesh, *Hannah Senesh: Her Life and Diary* (New York: Schocken Books, 1972).

18. *People*, 24 September 2001, p. 89.

19. *Time*, 24 September 2001, p. 75.

20. *USA Today*, 24 September 2001.

21. *Star*, 2 October 2001, p. 17.

22. *Newsweek*, 1 October 2001, p. 63.

23. *Star*, 2 October 2001, p. 5.

24. *World*, 29 September 2001, p. 12. Derek Jeter, New York Yankees shortstop, after visiting New York firefighters and rescue workers at the site of the fallen towers of the World Trade Center.

25. *U.S. News & World Report*, 24 September 2001, p. 42.

26. *National Enquirer*, 2 October 2001, pp. 12-13.

27. *Time*, 24 September 2001, pp. 70-71.

28. *Pioneer Press* (St. Paul), 16 September 2001.

29. Todd Brennan, "Where Have All the Heroes Gone?" *The Critic*, Fall 1976.

30. Felicia Hemans, from her poem *Casabianca*. Young Casabianca, a boy about thirteen years old, son of the Admiral of the Orient, remained at his post (in the Battle of the Nile) after the ship had taken fire and all the guns had been abandoned, and perished in the explosion of the vessel, when the flames had reached the powder.

31. *Washington Post*, 21 September 2001.

32. Hannah Senesh, *Hannah Senesh: Her Life and Diary* (New York: Schocken Books, 1972), p. 13.

33. Anne Frank, *The Diary of a Young Girl* (Englewood Cliffs, N.J.: Globe Book Co., 1992).

34. *Pioneer Press* (St. Paul), 16 September 2001.

35. *Time*, 24 September 2001, p. 75.

36. *CNN Larry King Live*, 18 September 2001.

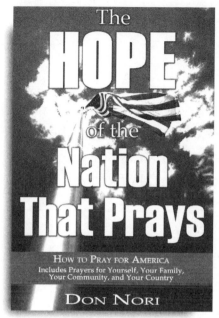

THE HOPE OF THE NATION THAT PRAYS
By Don Nori

The Hope of the Nation That Prays offers an encouraging look at God's love and His will for America. Will God answer our prayers? What prayers can we pray? What is God's will for America? What is God's will for me personally? Included are actual prayers for our country and for those we love, based upon Scriptures from the Bible.

Take a step back in time with prayers from historical figures who have experienced extraordinary answers to prayers in times of crisis. Featured, are prayers from such great leaders as George Washington, Martin Luther King Jr., Abraham Lincoln, and many others.

ISBN 0-7684-3045-3

Additional copies of this book and other
book titles from DESTINY IMAGE are
available at your local bookstore.

For a complete list of our titles,
visit us at www.destinyimage.com
Send a request for a catalog to:

Destiny Image® Publishers, Inc.

P.O. Box 310
Shippensburg, PA 17257-0310

*"Speaking to the Purposes of God for This
Generation and for the Generations to Come"*